Hurricane
Andrew

Titles in the *American Disasters* series:

The Exxon Valdez
Tragic Oil Spill
ISBN 0-7660-1058-9

Hurricane Andrew
Nature's Rage
ISBN 0-7660-1057-0

The Oklahoma City Bombing
Terror in the Heartland
ISBN 0-7660-1061-9

Plains Outbreak Tornadoes
Killer Twisters
ISBN 0-7660-1059-7

San Francisco Earthquake, 1989
Death and Destruction
ISBN 0-7660-1060-0

The World Trade Center Bombing
Terror in the Towers
ISBN 0-7660-1056-2

Hurricane Andrew

Nature's Rage

Victoria Sherrow

AMERICAN DISASTERS

Enslow Publishers, Inc.

44 Fadem Road   PO Box 38
Box 699   Aldershot
Springfield, NJ 07081   Hants GU12 6BP
USA   UK

Library of Congress Cataloging-in-Publication Data

Sherrow, Victoria.
    Hurricane Andrew: nature's rage / Victoria Sherrow.
        p. cm. — (American disasters)
    Includes bibliographical references and index.
    Summary: Details the course of Hurricane Andrew, which hit the
southeastern United States in 1992, and describes the recovery efforts
that followed the storm.
    ISBN 0-7660-1057-0
    1. Hurricane Andrew, 1992—Juvenile literature. 2. Hurricanes—
Florida—Juvenile literature. [1. Hurricane Andrew, 1992. 2. Hurricanes
—Florida.] I. Title. II. Series.
QC945.S485   1998
363.34'92281'097—dc21   97–39193
                                                    CIP
                                                      AC

Printed in the United States of America.

10 9 8 7 6 5 4 3 2 1

Photo Credits: AP/Wide World Photos, pp. 1, 6, 12, 13, 15, 18, 20, 22, 24, 27,
28, 29, 31, 32, 33, 34, 37, 40.

Cover Photo: AP/Wide World Photos

Contents

CHAPTER 1

Sheer Terror

Howling noises . . . weird purple streaks of lightning . . . blasts of wind . . . Then roofs torn off, doors and windows crashing, trees and boats flying through the air—sheer terror. This is how people remember Hurricane Andrew. It ripped through South Florida in August 1992.

"The front door opened, and wind came in like nothing I've seen before!" said one survivor. "We got soaking wet. Water went everywhere. The roof went off."[1]

Another person said, "Wind blew the glass in, then . . . —then I had the hurricane inside with me."[2]

One family in Coral Gables, Florida, stayed in their home during the storm. As wind and rain surged, they shoved a mattress against the door. But nothing could hold back this hurricane. Like so many other homes, this one was destroyed.

People have tried to describe the fierce winds that caused such damage. One man said they "sounded like a dozen freight trains on the loose."[3] A person can hardly stand up when the wind speed reaches sixty or seventy miles per hour. It can blow the shirt off your back. Hurricane Andrew brought winds more than twice that strong. People who felt those winds will never forget them. One person who felt them was Tim Tobin. "I was never so scared in all my life," he said later.[4] Tobin spent the hurricane crouched inside a building near Miami Beach. Three other men were there with him. One of them was in a wheelchair.

And after the storm? There was vast destruction, loss, and misery. People said South Florida looked like a war zone. Buildings had become piles of rubble. Groves of trees lay in tangled heaps. Planes at an airfield were "smashed like toys."[5] Stands of bleachers at a sports stadium had been blown off. Roads were cluttered with streetlights and telephone poles. People's homes, everything they had worked for, were ruined. "It was like twenty years was wiped out in two days," said one sixty-four-year-old woman.[6]

Florida is famous for its sunshine, orange trees, and resort areas. Visitors enjoy Disney World, Sea World, and the state's many beaches. But Florida is also prone to hurricanes—large, often violent storm systems. During these storms, there are winds of at least seventy-four miles per hour. People in this region have learned to live with hurricane warnings. Some have survived one or more of the deadly storms.

But Hurricane Andrew was a killer storm. It also became the costliest natural disaster in United States history. As one man said, "I've never been through one like this."[7]

CHAPTER 2

It's Coming Our Way

Hurricane Andrew was "the big one." For several years, some people had predicted that Florida was due for a serious storm. That August, they got that storm.

Years ago, people in the West Indies thought hurricanes were sent by the devil. The word *hurricane* comes from the West Indian word, *hurakán*, meaning "big wind." A Spanish sea captain, Fernández de Oviedo, heard this tale of the devil when he visited the West Indies. Then he spread this name to other countries. In a letter home, he wrote, "When the devil wishes to terrify [natives in the Caribbean], he promises them the "'Huracán' . . ."[1]

People in the Atlantic and eastern Pacific regions began calling these storms hurricanes. People in the western Pacific call them typhoons. This comes from the Greek word *typhon*, which means "violent storm."[2]

The National Hurricane Center (NHC) near Miami, Florida, has the job of watching out for these deadly storms. By Wednesday August 20, 1992, the NHC staff was on the alert. A tropical storm was swirling in the Atlantic Ocean. It was heading west, toward the southeastern United States.

The storm had begun far from Florida on August 14. An area of low pressure (called a tropical wave) had formed over western Africa. Then this wave moved westward to the tropical North Atlantic.

Before 1944, people had to rely on ships at sea or land weather stations to spot hurricanes. Since then, much better warning systems have been developed. Now, radar and weather satellites are always on guard. On August 16, those satellites showed pictures of the tropical wave from West Africa becoming a depression. This depression gathered speed over the next three days. It was starting to act like a hurricane.

Like most hurricanes in the North Atlantic, this one arose in the summer. The air is hot and moist and water temperatures are warm during summer months. These conditions favor hurricanes. Hurricane season usually ends by November. A few bad storms do occur at other times, however.

As the NHC tracked the storm, it suddenly turned north. The staff relaxed. Maybe this would be a quiet weekend, after all. Then the storm changed direction again. It moved west—right toward Florida. Bryan Norcross, a weatherman at WTVJ television in Miami, grew uneasy. He later said, "I didn't like the looks of this storm. I knew that soon someone within the sound of my voice was going to have a hurricane—and maybe a bad one."[3]

The water temperatures were warm. Ocean water must be at least 79° F for a hurricane to occur. The air temperatures were also warm. Only warm air can hold such large amounts of moisture. This storm gathered strength as it passed over the warm waters of the Caribbean.

Would this tropical storm explode into a hurricane? Satellite pictures showed storm clouds taking on a circular pattern. They were moving in a counterclockwise direction.

High-speed winds now surrounded an area of low pressure in the center of the storm. This low-pressure area is called the eye of the hurricane. It is a peaceful area in the center of the storm that measures about ten to thirty miles across. There, surface pressure is at its lowest. There are no clouds. Winds are light compared with the winds outside the eye. The difference in pressure between the eye and the area around it maintains the high speed of these outer winds.

On August 22, the storm reached hurricane strength. There was no longer any doubt. At 5:00 P.M. that day, the National Hurricane Center officially classified it as a hurricane.

The NHC began warning people that the hurricane would probably hit Florida. Radio and television announcers spread the word. They urged everyone to get out of the area—a complete evacuation. Schools and businesses

A satellite map shows Hurricane Andrew as it makes its way toward southern Florida.

shut down. Speaking through megaphones, police told people to leave their beach houses.

Most people in South Florida decided to play it safe. They fled before the storm hit land. Before leaving, they grabbed things they thought they might need while they were away.

By August 22, thousands of people were fleeing from South Florida. Traffic slowed as cars swarmed onto Highway 60. The airports were mobbed, too. At Miami

Workers at a restaurant in Miami Beach, Florida, tape windows and prepare a wooden cover for the front of the restaurant, as they get ready for Hurricane Andrew.

International Airport, ticket agent James Pierce recalled helping frantic customers. He said, "You would ask them where they want to go and they would say, 'Anywhere.' You could book them to Hong Kong, Germany—anywhere."[4]

In all, about fifty-five thousand people left the Florida Keys. Another 517,000 people left Dade County. Hundreds of thousands more Floridians left other counties. Some of these uprooted people stayed with friends or relatives. About forty-five thousand people crowded into emergency shelters. Others turned to hotels. Soon, hotels in the area filled up. People were told to go to Orlando, a city with many hotels, including those at Disney World.

Some people chose to stay home despite the danger and pleas from state officials. They were determined to "ride out the storm" and guard their property. A few others decided to spend the storm in their boats.

By now, this hurricane had a name—Andrew. In 1953, the National Weather Service began naming each hurricane. Each one received a woman's name, starting with Hurricane Hazel. Every letter in the alphabet was used. The use of men's names began in 1979.

Hurricane Andrew was small in size, but it was fierce. It reached peak strength. It became a category 4 hurricane when its eye passed over the Bahamas on August 23 and 24. A category 5 is the worst a hurricane can get.

The hurricane brought heavy rains. As hurricanes form, the rain releases heat. This maintains the low central pressure and the strong winds. The cloud systems of a tropical storm can become huge. Some have measured nearly two thousand miles across.

Over the radio, people in Florida heard the scared voices of people in the Bahamas who had seen Hurricane Andrew. By Sunday evening, Andrew was less than twelve hours away. This meant it would probably hit Florida at high tide, causing severe water damage.

People in Florida made final preparations. On Sunday, police discovered more than two hundred elderly people, many in wheelchairs, stranded at a nursing home in

*H*urricane Andrew's devastating winds and driving rains destroyed everything in their path.

Homestead. Five of these people were moved to a local hospital. The police quickly searched for buses to carry the rest to a shelter.

The shelter was at a local school in Richmond Heights. Classrooms, auditoriums, and hallways were already crowded with more than one thousand people. Some of them helped the police and nurses to carry in the frightened elderly patients. They set up the patients' wheelchairs inside the building. Other people rested on blankets on the floor. No food, medical supplies, or water had arrived yet.

Now people all over South Florida could only watch and wait. Each hour brought the hurricane closer. For the people in Andrew's path, the next few days would change their lives.

CHAPTER 3

In the Monster's Path

Shortly before 5:00 A.M. on August 24, Hurricane Andrew hit southern Dade County, Florida. The storm had weakened a little. It regained strength just before it hit land, however. When it finally hit, Andrew was again a severe, category 4 hurricane.

Andrew roared across the land, smashing, crushing, and soaking whatever it touched. Buildings were torn to pieces. Chunks of glass, wood, plaster, and stone flew into the air. So did whole cars, Dumpsters, and trees. Many people agreed with a woman who said, "I thought the house was going to blow away."[1]

The rain pounded down in thick streams of water. Then there were the loud howling noises. Some people said they sounded like bombs. These noises came from winds moving at speeds of 140 miles per hour. Gusts were measured at up to 170 miles per hour.

Andrew had hit land at high tide. A tidal surge twelve feet high caused a great deal of damage. Waves of water toppled trees, flattened homes, and wrecked the Homestead Air Force Base.

People inside the school shelter at Richmond Heights felt Andrew's fury. Most of them had been too nervous to fall asleep. Now they heard the sounds of wind-borne objects slapping the doors, windows, and walls. People screamed or wept as ceilings collapsed and rain gushed inside.

Soon, more people from the town arrived at this shelter. A newspaper reporter arrived. He wrote of those

A storm-damaged F-16 fighter plane shows the effects of high winds, after Hurricane Andrew passed through Homestead Air Force Base.

inside: "They are dripping wet, muddy, and many of them burst into tears as they arrive inside."[2]

Four members of the Baldwin family huddled together inside their home, waiting. Outside, winds tore off their roof and blew out the windows. The home was destroyed, but the family was safe. Richard New thought the motel where he lived was strong enough to hold up during a hurricane. He was in for a shock. The windowpanes popped out, and New raced for the closet. Then, fierce winds knocked out his window air conditioner. He said, "Everything started to shudder all over the neighborhood."[3]

Betty Vale was in a concrete house, but even those walls began to shake. She said, "It sounded like a poltergeist or the devil himself was out there trying to break in. I'll never forget that horrible sound. It went on for hours."[4]

A family of seven in Perrine stayed in their house that night. They ran to a different room each time the windows shattered. Eventually, every window was gone. The adults held a mattress over the children, and they all rushed into the bathroom. They were terrified that the bathroom would cave in, too.

Other families also decided the bathroom was the safest place to hide. A family of five crowded into this small space with their dog. One child sat holding the dog in the tub. Already, their roof and doors had been ripped off. For four hours, they prayed.

One of their neighbors saw the top disappear from a

A man stands in what was once his bedroom, after
Hurricane Andrew made its way through the area.

large tree in his yard. He said, "It was like a magic hand
just clipped the top of it off."[5]

Like many people in Homestead, April Counts lived in
a trailer. A disabled veteran was with her during the hurricane. They did not know they were supposed to leave
the area. When Andrew struck, the trailer began to snap
apart. Counts helped her friend outside. Tensely, they
waited in the backseat of her car. Amazingly, the car held
up, as everything around them was destroyed.

By this time, wind speeds were more than 120 miles
per hour. Small whirlwinds also formed near the center of
the storm. These whirlwinds gained speed as they were
pulled inward. Many strong gusts added to the power of

Hurricane Andrew. They increased the wind force. It raged at more than two hundred miles per hour in some places.

Andrew continued on its destructive path. Radar equipment and wind vanes were knocked down. These instruments recorded wind speeds of 164 miles per hour before they stopped working. Winds this strong can whip slabs of concrete into the air. They can demolish a house in seconds.

One television station stayed on the air during that incredible morning. Channel 4 weather forecaster Bryan Norcross spent more than twenty hours on camera. By 6:00 A.M., Norcross was able to tell viewers that Andrew had left South Florida. The storm had not done major damage to heavily populated Miami or wealthy, mansion-filled Palm Beach.

Hurricane Andrew now streaked across the Gulf of Mexico toward Louisiana. The hurricane strengthened as it crossed the warm waters in the Gulf. More than 1 million people fled from southeastern and south-central Louisiana.

A television reporter inspected the town of Jeanerette just before Andrew struck. The main street was deserted—almost. The reporter said the family that owned the hardware store was "sitting in lawn chairs as though they're waiting for a parade."[6] He told a city official, "You've obviously got a lot of people who decided to stay and weather it through."[7] Some shrimp fishermen had tied their boats to the banks. They planned to spend the storm in the boats.

For a while, it seemed that the hurricane would strike heavily populated New Orleans. But it made landfall west of Morgan City at 5:00 A.M. on August 26. This coastal area is known for its sugarcane plantations.

Now people in Louisiana felt Andrew's fury. Charley McKinley was in his mother's house in Patterson. He heard the nails popping out of the roof. McKinley ran toward a neighbor's house. He said that the walls of that house were "expandin' like they was breathin'."[8]

In New Iberia, a high school served as a shelter.

*T*he powerful winds of Hurricane Andrew wrecked havoc on Florida City, Florida. The water tower is all that remains standing.

Hundreds of people heard the wind moaning. Then, said one, "the rains and winds came. The roof was destroyed and the water poured in."[9] Another woman spent the storm in a hotel. She remembered, "Everything was coming this way, so we were hanging on to the back of each other's jackets. Now I'm going to cry."[10]

Mabel's Lounge, a pool hall, stayed open all night. The owner bought extra groceries and invited people to gather there during the storm. They worked together putting sandbags around the building. Mabel recalled the storm itself: "the wind, the wind—the water, the wind."[11]

Afterward, Andrew was weaker but still dangerous. Tornadoes damaged buildings and caused more deaths. Flooding occurred in many places. More than seven inches of rain fell in southeast Florida, Louisiana, and Mississippi. About five inches fell in neighboring states. Hammond, Louisiana, reported the heaviest rainfall—11.92 inches.

On August 26, Hurricane Andrew was downgraded to a tropical storm. The storm had lost power as it joined with a cold front moving east. It turned into a series of heavy rains and strong winds. Finally, the fury that had been Hurricane Andrew faded out over Pennsylvania.

Emergency crews now headed for the stricken areas. Nervous residents prepared to return home. What would they find there?

CHAPTER 4

We Have Nothing

Skies remained gray and rain fell as the hurricane left. Andrew was a rather compact hurricane and its path had been narrow. As a result, it looked as if a tornado, not a hurricane, had struck.

The eye of the storm was inland for less than four hours. Yet the area was devastated. Buildings and homes lay in ruins. Fierce winds had lifted boats out of marinas. Cars and trucks had been smashed or blown on top of buildings. Phone lines and wires were down.

The American Red Cross (ARC) set up shelters to receive victims. A Red Cross spokesman called the situation critical. He said, "If you put Hurricane Hugo and the 1989 San Francisco area earthquake together and doubled the magnitude of the damage, that's what we have."[1] In all, about fifteen thousand Red Cross workers would help victims over the next four months.[2]

After the storm, many people returned home. They had to find out what remained. Al Scott and his family discovered the whole roof was gone from their house in Kendall. Everything inside the house had been blown away. Scott's young son asked, "Dad, what happened to our things?"[3]

Other families also looked for their belongings. Some were able to retrieve some objects in the rubble—a book, a small appliance, a toy, a piece of clothing.

Many found that nothing was left. One woman said that when she saw her apartment, "I went crazy. That's all I had." She could hardly bear to look inside. Pointing at the ruins, she said, "All your life, you work hard, to get a little something, to live comfortable. . . ."[4]

Another victim told a TV news crew, "We have nothing, nothing at all." A neighbor said in despair, "I don't know what we're going to do."[5]

Farmers lost their livestock, crops, or both. A Thai-American woman living near the Everglades lost her trailer and her crops. She had spent three years planting fruits to sell to grocery stores. All five acres of trees were gone. She said, "I felt so sad. So hurt. I worked so hard. I had 320 banana trees. Many guavas and litchis. . . . Why did this have to happen?"[6]

People suffered in many other ways. Rescue workers with dogs combed fallen buildings for injured people. The number of injured rose each day. People had different kinds of injuries. They had broken bones, infections, and pieces of glass lodged in their feet.

Victims were brought to area hospitals and emergency clinics. Medical workers from other states came to help.

More than a dozen people were reported dead. Some were crushed in collapsed buildings. Others were hit by heavy flying objects. Police patrolled the streets to help survivors and stop looting. They imposed a 7:00 P.M. curfew. The National Guard was also sent to stop looting. Stealing from homes and stores had begun the day after the hurricane. Thieves helped themselves to television sets, radios, VCRs, clothing, shoes, guns, toys, and other things. They snatched a vacuum cleaner and sewing

*P*eople line up outside a grocery store, waiting for free food and other items. The store was giving away what it had managed to save from the storm.

A member of the Florida National Guard walks through the debris left behind by Hurricane Andrew. The National Guard was called out to prevent looting.

machine from the ruins of April Counts's trailer. She later described how angry she felt: "You've already lost what you had. And they steal what you have left."[7]

Valerie Vernon was a forty-one-year-old grandmother who lived in South Miami Heights. She said, "There were guys running around with shopping carts loaded up with food. . . . It was disgusting."[8]

People waited for the Red Cross to bring water and other help. Hungry, thirsty people lined up at buildings that had been chosen as relief centers. They picked up jugs of water and cans of food. Many people had to walk more than a mile in the hot sun.

Some people complained that help was coming too

slowly. There were not enough emergency shelters or working phones. Kate Hale was Dade County's director of emergency services. She said, "We need food. We need water. We need people. For God's sake, where are they?"[9]

Up to 250,000 people were temporarily homeless, with 25,524 homes gone and 101,241 homes damaged. In southern Dade County, 90 percent of all the mobile homes were destroyed. Only nine of the 1,176 mobile homes in Homestead were left.

It was clear that local and state relief efforts alone could not handle this catastrophe. Federal agencies were called to the scene. In the end, more federal aid was given to help victims of this disaster than ever before.

President George Bush visited the scene. Afterward,

*P*resident George Bush (center) with Florida governor Lawton Chiles (left), checks on areas devastated by Hurricane Andrew.

he spoke to the nation. He thanked Americans for helping the victims of Hurricane Andrew. He encouraged people to donate money to the Red Cross. Americans responded generously. Within a single day, more than fifty-three thousand people sent contributions. More than $4 million was collected.

Officials warned survivors that dangers still existed. Twenty-six people had died directly from the storm. The indirect deaths brought that number to sixty-five. People can die after hurricanes for various reasons. Bridges and roads may weaken, causing auto accidents. Poisonous substances may reach the water supply, leading to illness and death.

Eighteen deaths were reported from accidents after Hurricane Andrew. Most were from fires, electrocutions, and falls. A thirty-three-year-old man died while working on an electrical pole. Another was electrocuted when he touched a live wire while trying to clean up his yard. Two others died while climbing on their roofs. Two children died in a home fire. The family had been using a candle for light. It fell over and ignited the room.

People's lives were turned upside down after the hurricane. Meeting basic needs—shelter, food, water, keeping clean—was a daily struggle. Many people said they were grateful just to have a place to sleep and something to eat.

A Red Cross volunteer said, "We had two elderly women yesterday—eight-five and eighty-seven. Their home had been flattened; they hadn't eaten in three days.

A worried father (right) waits while his children brush their teeth at a tent city for the homeless victims of Hurricane Andrew.

Another lady just left here with three . . . kids. And no home, no food."[10]

During the day, long lines formed at social service centers. People filled out forms that would help them get money for repairs. They became frustrated by these long waits.

Many parts of southern Florida lacked telephone and postal services. People there read the newspapers carefully. They were looking for lists of the services that were available for hurricane victims. They also used the papers to pass on messages to relatives, friends, and employers. Some 2.5 million people were without power.[11] Some people

A young girl is comforted by a Florida National Guardsman. She and her family were forced to take refuge in this tent city after their home was destroyed.

lacked these services for a matter of days. For others, the inconvenience lasted for months.

Housing was, of course, a major concern. Some people went north to take rooms in hotels. Others moved in with relatives. People whose homes were still standing tried to repair them. They removed debris, dried out rooms, and covered holes in roofs with tar paper. Trucks carried water to people living in places where the water was not safe to drink.

Thousands of homeless people were forced to stay in tent cities. These shelters had been set up by the Red Cross. The largest tent city was located in Homestead. It sat on what had once been Harris Field at the air force base.

Tent cities became crowded and muddy, and diseases spread easily. Children suffered from earaches, ringworm, and bug bites. People complained about the swarms of mosquitoes. These annoying insects thrived in the warm, humid climate.

A lack of privacy brought more discomfort. There were no bathrooms. People were assigned times when they could take showers. Portable toilets served hundreds of people.

About twenty-five thousand people moved away from Florida after Hurricane Andrew. The poorest residents tended to stay behind because they had nowhere else to go. Those who did remain would spend months, even years, rebuilding their lives.

Life changed drastically for victims of Hurricane Andrew. These people wait in line for food at a tent city.

CHAPTER 5

A Long Recovery

Life after Hurricane Andrew was filled with losses. People had to adjust to these losses and to the changes in everyday life. Some were also recovering from injuries or health problems caused by the storm. Many mourned pets that had been lost or had run away.

These disaster victims had to do without many things other Americans take for granted. Watching television, buying a hamburger, using a hair dryer, taking a warm bath, or making a phone call were no longer possible. These people longed to sleep in their own beds. Instead they had only a cot in a tent with strangers.

Their day-to-day activities were quite different, too. Some had no transportation. Many cars had been destroyed. People lost time at work. Some even lost their jobs. For others, their workplaces no longer existed. Many people said life had spun "out of control." One woman voiced the thoughts of many others. She asked a television commentator, "Where do I go from here?"[1]

Jane Baldwin described her problems as secretary at the First Baptist Church in Cutler Ridge in South Dade County:

> The focus was on trying to find our people, trying to minister to our people; trying to locate records, work without copy machines, without telephones, without typewriters, without computers, and it was overwhelming. . . .[2]

Young people had special problems of their own. Schools that were badly damaged had to be shut down. Temporary schools were set up in different places. Children missed their familiar schools. There were no sports to play, and playgrounds were gone. Young people also lost friends when families moved to other places to live or work.

College student Melanie Baldwin dropped out of school. For a while, she tried working at three different jobs. She said, "Everything's so unstable. Before the storm, you know . . . I was just very secure in everything, and then, all of a sudden, everything changed."[3]

Mental health workers tried to help people cope with the stress caused by the hurricane. Dr. Diane Blank, a psychologist, helped people in Dade County. She said that it was important for people to "see somebody who cares. . . . The job of mental health volunteers is to offer a sense of human caring, human contact in the middle of all the red tape, all the confusion."[4]

Other people also came to help. Some volunteers came from South Carolina. They could really sympathize with

Volunteer spirit was evident in many places following Hurricane Andrew. These volunteers are unloading emergency supplies from a military helicopter.

the victims because they had lived through Hurricane Hugo three years before, in 1989. Other Americans headed for Florida on their own. They offered their skills as carpenters, roofers, or forklift operators. Some volunteers cooked and served food or looked after children in church relief centers.

Many victims expressed despair. People called Hurricane Andrew a nightmare. Others said it was worse than anything else they could imagine. People also said they were determined not to let the disaster destroy them. Some talked about things they could feel good about. "I thank God my family is safe," said Millie Romero of Perrine, Florida. "We pulled through this together."[5]

Counselors continued to work with victims months after the hurricane ended. Dr. Charles Gibbs, a psychologist, counseled victims. He told a reporter that survivors were feeling strong emotions.

> There's a lot of anxiety, restlessness, and an increase in anger and irritability—all of which is a perfectly normal response to a disaster of this magnitude. Many of the children are suffering night terrors. They see "Andrew" as a real person and they're afraid he's coming back, that he's going to kill them.[6]

Parents noticed signs of stress in their children. Young ones went back to wetting the bed and sucking their thumbs. Many mourned the loss of special toys and belongings that could not be replaced. Some had nightmares. They were afraid that another hurricane would come and kill them. Some kept watching the sky. They would become upset when they saw clouds. Parents spent a great deal of time comforting their children. One seven-year-old said, "I think it's coming back. I'm gonna cry, cry, cry."[7]

Counselors helped children express their anger. They talked with a mean-looking puppet they named "Andrew." Children met in groups to share their feelings.

Patricia Regester was the director of the Mental Health Association in Dade County. She pointed out that people would probably be healing for a long time. She said, "We've got years and years of rebuilding people. Not just the buildings. We've got to deal with the people damage."[8]

Hurricane Andrew was the most expensive disaster in United States history. The damage totaled more than $25 billion. Most of that damage was in Florida. There was about $1 billion worth of damage in Louisiana and $0.25 billion in the Bahamas. Another $0.5 billion occurred in the Gulf of Mexico. In the gulf, thirteen oil platforms toppled. Five platforms were leaning. Twenty satellite dishes toppled, and twenty-three were leaning. There were 104 incidents of structural damage, seven incidents of pollution, and two fires. Five drilling wells were blown off location.[9]

The hurricane had destroyed 25,524 homes. Over one hundred thousand others were damaged. There was massive damage to buildings and crops in Mississippi and Louisiana. The sugarcane crop was especially hard hit. About 167,000 homes and businesses in Louisiana were left without electricity.[10] Boat losses totaled half a billion dollars.

There was also damage offshore. An artificial reef system near Florida was affected. *The St. Petersburg Times* reported that the hurricane destroyed 33 percent of the coral reefs at Biscayne National Park.[11] Andrew took down 90 percent of the native pines, mangroves, and tropical hardwood trees.

Recovery after such a huge disaster took a long time. Seven months after Andrew struck, some neighborhoods still looked much as they did right after the storm. Bob Edwards is a host for National Public Radio. He reported that many homes still had "roofs blown off, windows missing, walls caved in."[12] Others were still being

*T*his owner of the Everglades Alligator Farm tries to keep newborn alligators warm in a bathtub. Storm damage claimed the alligator's usual home.

repaired. Reporter Derek Reveron said some homes in the Cutler Ridge area of southern Dade County were "gutted shells."[13]

A year later, residents of some stricken areas were still struggling to rebuild. Federal relief agencies and volunteers continued to provide services. The Red Cross is one example. They operated a disaster service center in Homestead for four months after the storm. Some Red Cross workers remained in the area for a full year. The total cost of the Red Cross relief operation was about $84 million.

Many people in southern Florida had been struggling

to make ends meet even before the storm struck. Now they had even more problems. However, some took advantage of the social services they were offered. They were able to enroll in school for more education. Some found better jobs than they had before.

These people were used to taking care of themselves. They felt embarrassed when they continued to need help, month after month. Becky Spillers said, "It's really hard to accept gifts or people giving you money. We have a hard time accepting the fact that we're disaster victims. . . . It's really hard to accept that you really are unemployed and have no income."[14]

Some problems remained years after the storm. As of 1997, five years after Andrew's wrath, three hundred people were still on waiting lists for home repairs or rebuilding.[15] Homestead Air Force Base had been turned into a reserve base. This caused a loss of eleven thousand jobs in the local economy.

Survivor Lisa Swindell says, "Andrew changed everyone's outlook as far as what's really important in life."[16] Bill Spillers was sure that someday life would again be "normal." But he thinks that people change after this kind of crisis. "I don't know how to predict when it will be normal for me," he said.[17]

Many hurricane survivors agreed that the experience changed them. Some described a new respect for the forces of nature. Others spoke of their lingering fears. People also felt a lot of anger. But a hurricane is not a person that can be confronted.

As bad as Andrew was, scientists say it could have been much worse. According to the National Weather Service, "Andrew was a compact system. A little larger system, or one making landfall just a few nautical miles further to the north, would have been catastrophic . . ." Miami, Miami Beach, Key Biscayne, and Fort Lauderdale have much larger populations. There are more hotels, businesses, and factories there than in the area that was hit the hardest.

Fewer lives were lost than is usual with a storm as ferocious as Andrew. This is because the weather service could act quickly. It is often hard to predict the path of a hurricane. Scientists had an easier time with Andrew. The National Weather Service spotted it early. They were able to forecast its movements. People were removed from the most dangerous areas. Being prepared saved lives.

Since Andrew hit, more coastal areas than ever have been developed as residential areas. By the late 1990s, millions of people lived in areas that hurricanes may hit. There were more hurricanes than usual, too. In 1995, nineteen tropical storms produced thirteen hurricanes. In 1996, nine of thirteen tropical storms became hurricanes.

The people who lived through Hurricane Andrew say that nobody can really know what it is like to go through a disaster unless it happens to them. Valerie Vernon says, "I remember sitting and watching Hurricane Hugo on TV, but it never occurred to me what it actually does to people's lives."[18]

Other Significant Hurricanes

UNITED STATES				
YEAR	NAME	PLACE	DEAD	DAMAGE
1900	*	Galveston, Texas area	6,000	Unknown
1915	*	Mississippi Delta	275	Unknown
1935	*	Florida (Keys)	over 400	Unknown
1938	*	Long Island and New England	600	$400 million
1954	Hurricane Hazel	North and South Carolina	1,173	$281 million
1955	Hurricane Diane	North Carolina to New England	184	$1.75 billion
1957	Hurricane Audrey	Louisiana, Mississippi, Texas	550	$150 million
1965	Hurricane Betsy	Louisiana, Florida, Bahamas	76	$1.42 billion
1969	Hurricane Camille	Mississippi, Louisiana	256	$1.42 billion
1972	Hurricane Agnes	Florida to New York	122	$3 billion
1979	Hurricane Frederic	Alabama and Mississippi	8	$1.5 billion
1989	Hurricane Hugo	West Indies and southeastern U.S.	60	$10 billion
1992	Hurricane Inike	Hawaiian Island of Kauai	7	$2 billion
WORLDWIDE				
YEAR	NAME	PLACE	DEAD	DAMAGE
1906	Typhoon	Hong Kong	10,000	Unknown
1928	Hurricane	Caribbean, South Florida	4,000	Unknown
1930	Hurricane	Santa Domingo	2,000	Unknown
1934	Typhoon	Honshu, Japan	4,000	Unknown
1942	Typhoon	Bengal, India	40,000	Unknown
1963	Hurricane Flora	Haiti, Cuba, Dominican Republic	over 7,100	Unknown
1974	Hurricane Fifi	Honduras	8,000	$1 billion
1984	Hurricane Ike	Southern Philippines	1,363	Unknown
1988	Hurricane Gilbert	Caribbean, Gulf of Mexico	800	$10 billion

*Hurricanes were not given names until 1953.

Chapter 1. Sheer Terror

1. "Hurricane Andrew," *48 Hours*, CBS News, August 26, 1992. Burrelle's Transcript, p. 21.

2. Ibid.

3. Ibid., pp. 9–10.

4. Jim Sams and Michael J. Spencer, "Survival Techniques: 'It Floats When It's Underwater, Too," *Sarasota Herald-Tribune*, August 25, 1992.

5. Rick Gore, "Andrew Aftermath," *National Geographic*, April 1993, p. 9.

6. Jim Sams and Michael J. Spencer, "Defeated Store Owner Fears Homestead's End," *Sarasota Herald-Tribune*, August 26, 1992, p. 1.

7. Quoted in "Hurricane Andrew," *48 Hours*, CBS News, Burrelle's Transcript, p. 5.

Chapter 2. It's Coming Our Way

1. Gary Lockart, *The Weather Companion* (New York: John Wiley & Sons, Inc. 1988), p. 102.

2. Rick Gore, "Andrew Aftermath," *National Geographic*, April 1993, p. 14.

3. Chris Lavin, et al., "Hurricane Andrew," *St. Petersburg Times*, August 25, 1992, p. 1.

4. As quoted in a diary compiled by staff writers Chris Lavin, Anne V. Hull, Charlotte Sutton, Bill Adair, David Olinger, Susan Benesch, and Craig Pittman for the *St. Petersburg Times*, August 29, 1996.

Chapter 3. In the Monster's Path

1. Michael J. Spencer and Jim Sams, "Cramped Bathrooms Offer Safe Harbor," *Sarasota Herald-Tribune*, August 25, 1992, p. 1A.

2. Chris Levin, et al., "Hurricane Andrew," *St. Petersburg Times*, August 25, 1992, p. 1.

3. Jim Sams and Michael J. Spencer, "Survival Techniques: 'It Floats When It's Underwater, Too," *Sarasota Herald-Tribune*, August 25, 1992, p. 1A.

4. Rick Gore, "Andrew Aftermath," *National Geographic*, April 1993, p. 22.

5. Sams and Spencer, "Survival Techniques," p. 1A.

6. Quoted in "Hurricane Andrew," *48 Hours*, CBS News, August 26, 1992. Burrelle's Transcript, p. 7.

7. Ibid., p. 8.

8. Gore, p. 35.

9. "Hurricane Andrew," *48 Hours*, p. 10.

10. Ibid.

11. Ibid., p. 27.

Chapter 4. We Have Nothing

1. Quoted in Rick Gore, "Andrew Aftermath," *National Geographic*, April 1993, p. 15.

2. "Hurricane Andrew Results in One of the Most Comprehensive Disaster Relief Efforts in Red Cross History," fact sheet, American Red Cross, 1993.

3. Chris Lavin, et al., "Hurricane Andrew," *St. Petersburg Times*, August 25, 1992, p. 1.

4. "Hurricane Andrew," *48 Hours*, CBS News, August 26, 1992. Burrelle's Transcript, p. 12.

5. Ibid., p. 22.

6. Quoted in Gore, p. 25.

7. Diane Lacey Allen, "The Story of Three Families," *Psychology Today*, November/December 1992, p. 40.

8. Ibid., p. 92.

9. Gore, p. 20.

10. Ibid., p. 23.

11. National Disaster Survey Report, "Hurricane Andrew: South Florida and Louisiana, August 23–26, 1992."

Chapter 5. A Long Recovery

1. Quoted in "Hurricane Andrew," *48 Hours*, CBS News, August 26, 1992. Burrelle's Transcript, p. 12.

2. Bob Edwards, Morning Edition, National Public Radio (NPR), April 2, 1993.

3. Ibid.

4. James Mauro, "Hurricane Andrew's Other Legacy," *Psychology Today*, November–December 1992, p. 93.

5. Ibid., p. 42.

6. Michael J. Spencer and Jim Sams, "Cramped Bathrooms Offer Safe Harbor," *Sarasota Herald-Tribune*, August 25, 1992, p. 12A.

7. Rick Gore, "Andrew Aftermath," *National Geographic*, April 1993, p. 10.

8. Quoted in Diane Lacey Allen, "The Story of Three Families," *Psychology Today*, November/December 1992, p. 92.

9. P. J. Hebert, J. D. Jarrell, and M. Mayfield, "The Deadliest, Costliest, and Most Intense Hurricane of This Century," NOAA Technical Memorandum NWS NHC-31 (Washington, D.C.: National Oceanic and Atmospheric Administration, U.S. Department of Commerce, 1992).

10. Ibid.

11. Chris Lavin, et al., "Hurricane Andrew," *St. Petersburg Times*, August 25, 1992, p. 1.

12. Edwards, Morning Edition.

13. Derek Reveron, Morning Edition, National Public Radio, April 2, 1993.

14. Quoted in Allen, p. 40.

15. Deborah Sharp, "5 Years After Andrew, Fla. Towns Still Struggle," *USA Today*, June 2, 1997, p. 7A.

16. Ibid.

17. Allen, p. 92.

18. Ibid.

American Red Cross—A relief organization founded by Clara Barton, a volunteer nurse during the Civil War. It helps victims of wars and natural disasters.

cyclone—A violent windstorm in which masses of air rotate rapidly around a low-pressure center.

debris—Bits and pieces that remain scattered after things are broken or destroyed.

eye (of a hurricane)—The center of a hurricane. It has no clouds and light winds.

gust—A sudden, powerful rush of wind.

hurricane—A storm that originates over tropical waters in the Atlantic Ocean, with heavy rains and violent winds that exceed seventy-four miles per hour. (*See also* typhoon.)

National Hurricane Center (NHC)—This government weather center in Miami, Florida, watches for tropical storms that may develop into hurricanes. The NHC issues hurricane warnings.

radar—A device that uses radio waves to find and track objects. It uses reflected radio waves.

typhoon—A storm that originates over tropical waters in the Pacific Ocean, with heavy rains and violent winds that exceed seventy-four miles per hour. (*See also* hurricane.)

weather satellite—A spacecraft that orbits Earth. It can be equipped with instruments that can transmit photos of clouds and storm patterns to stations that track the weather.

Books:

Archer, Jules. *Hurricane!* Parsippany, N.J.: Silver Burdett Press, 1991.

Canning, John, ed. *Great Disasters: Catastrophes of the Twentieth Century.* New York: Gallery Books, 1967.

Cleary, Margot Keam. *Great Disasters of the 20th Century.* New York: Gallery Books, 1990.

Davis, Lee. *Natural Disasters.* New York: Facts on File, 1992.

Gardner, Robert, and David Webster. *Science Projects About Weather.* Hillside, N.J.: Enslow Publishers, Inc., 1994.

Greenberg, Keith. *Hurricanes and Tornadoes.* New York: Twenty-First Century Books, 1994.

Keller, David. *Great Disasters: The Most Shocking Moments in History.* New York: Byron Press, 1990.

Lampton, Christopher. *Hurricane.* Brookfield, Conn.: The Millbrook Press, 1992.

Twist, Clint. *Hurricanes and Storms.* Parsippany, N.J.: Silver Burdett Press, 1992.

Magazine Articles

Eliot, John L. "Into the Eye of David," *National Geographic,* September 1980, pp. 368–379.

Funk, Ben. "Hurricane!" *National Geographic,* September 1980, pp. 346–356; 363–367.

The Internet

National Hurricane Center

>http://nhc-hp3.nhc.noaa.gov/index.html<

National Weather Service

>http://www.nws.noaa.gov/tpc/andrewpr.html<

Red Cross

>http//www.redcross.org/hec/1980-present/andrew.html<